LOOKING AT
COUNTRIES

Looking at
ISRAEL

Kathleen Pohl

Reading consultant: Susan Nations, M.Ed.,
author/literacy coach/consultant in literacy development

Gareth Stevens
Publishing

Please visit our Web site at www.garethstevens.com.
For a free color catalog describing Gareth Stevens Publishing's list of
high-quality books, call 1-800-542-2595 (USA) or 1-800-387-3178 (Canada).
Gareth Stevens Publishing's fax: 1-877-542-2596

Library of Congress Cataloging-in-Publication Data

Pohl, Kathleen.
    Looking at Israel / Kathleen Pohl.
       p. cm—(Looking at Countries)
Includes bibliographical references and index.
  ISBN-10: 0-8368-8770-0   ISBN-13: 978-0-8368-8770-9 (lib. bdg.)
  ISBN-10: 0-8368-8777-8   ISBN-13: 978-0-8368-8777-8 (softcover)
1. Israel—Juvenile literature. I. Title
DS1265P618 2008
956.94—dc22   207039847

This edition first published in 2008 by
Gareth Stevens Publishing
A Weekly Reader® Company
1 Reader's Digest Road
Pleasantville, NY 10570-7000 USA

Copyright © 2008 by Gareth Stevens, Inc.

Senior Managing Editor: Lisa M. Guidone
Senior Editor: Barbara Bakowski
Creative Director: Lisa Donovan
Designer: Tammy West
Photo Researcher: Sylvia Ohlrich

Photo credits: (t=top, b=bottom)
Cover Age Fotostock; title page Alberto Biscaro/Masterfile; p. 4 Ohad Shahar/Alamy; p. 6 Richard Ashworth/
Getty Images; p. 7t Sylvain Grandadam/Age Fotostock; p. 7b D. Usher/Peter Arnold; p. 8 Haim Azulay/
Reuters/Landov; p. 9t Duby Tal/Alamy; p. 9b Hanan Isachar/Corbis; p. 10 Gil Cohen Magen/Reuters/Landov;
p. 11t Shutterstock; p. 11b Ammar Awad/Reuters/Landov; p. 12t Nayeff Hashlamoun/Reuters/Landov;
p. 12b Debbie Hill/UPI/Landov; p. 13 Gadi Geffen/Israel Images/Alamy; p. 14 Jon Arnold Images/SuperStock;
p. 15t Victor de Schwanberg/Alamy; p. 15b R. Matina/Age Fotostock; p. 16 George Simhoni/Masterfile;
p. 17t Niall Benvie/Corbis; p. 17b Jacky Costi/Alamy; p. 18 Israel Images/Alamy; p. 19t Israel Images/Alamy;
p. 19b Christine Osborne Pictures/Alamy; p. 20t Tim Hill/Alamy; p. 20b George Simhoni/Masterfile;
p. 21t Jon Arnold Images/SuperStock; p. 21b Richard Nowitz/Israel Images/Alamy; p. 22 Mark Boulton/Alamy;
p. 23t David Silverman/Getty Images; p. 23b Israel Images/Alamy; p. 24 Cris Haigh/Getty Images;
p. 25t Eddie Gerald/Bloomberg/Landov; p. 25b Edi Israel/Israel Sun/Landov; p. 26 SuperStock; p. 27t SuperStock;
p. 27b Eitan Simanor/Alamy

Printed in the United States of America

1 2 3 4 5 6 7 8 9 10 09 08 07

Contents

Words that appear in the glossary are printed in **boldface** type the first time they occur in the text.

Where Is Israel?

Israel is in southwestern Asia, in a part of the world called the Middle East. Israel shares borders with four other countries. Those countries are Egypt to the southwest, Jordan and Syria to the east, and Lebanon to the north. Israel is shaped like a long, thin arrow. Its southern tip lies on the Red Sea. Israel also has a coast on the Mediterranean Sea.

Did you know?

Even though Israel is small, its land is varied. The country has deserts, mountains, valleys, and coastlines.

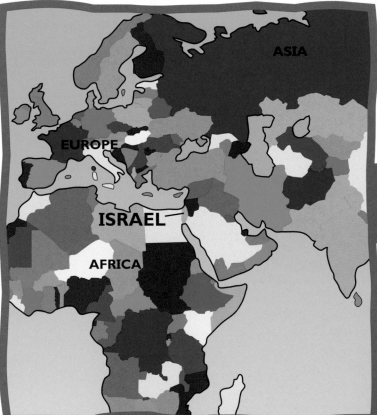

Israel is in a part of the world known as the Middle East.

Israel's lawmakers meet in this building in Jerusalem, the capital.

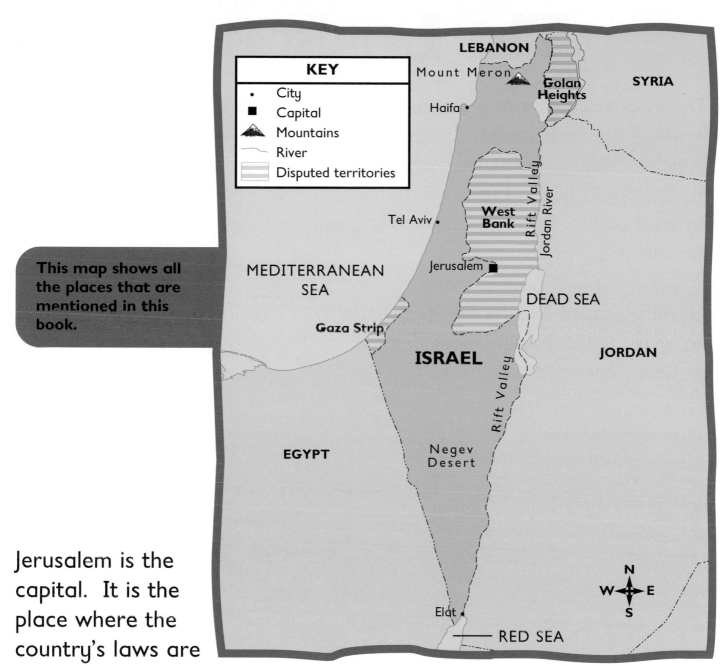

KEY

- • City
- ■ Capital
- ▲ Mountains
- ～ River
- ▨ Disputed territories

LEBANON

Mount Meron

Golan Heights

SYRIA

Haifa •

Tel Aviv •

West Bank

Rift Valley

Jordan River

MEDITERRANEAN SEA

Jerusalem ■

DEAD SEA

Gaza Strip

JORDAN

ISRAEL

Rift Valley

EGYPT

Negev Desert

N
W E
S

Elat •

RED SEA

This map shows all the places that are mentioned in this book.

Jerusalem is the capital. It is the place where the country's laws are made. People have lived in Jerusalem for more than four thousand years. It has old streets and buildings. It also has modern offices, shops, and restaurants.

Israel has hardly been at peace since the country was founded in 1948. It has fought with nearby countries for control of important land areas.

The Landscape

The **coastal plain** is a flat piece of land on the west coast. It has sandy beaches along the Mediterranean Sea. Most Israelis live in big cities on the coastal plain. Some of the land is good for farming.

Mountains and hills make up most of northern and central Israel. The highest peak is Mount Meron, in the

Did you know?

The shore of the Dead Sea is the lowest place on Earth's surface.

The Dead Sea is really a saltwater lake. The salt forms strange shapes on the shoreline.

The Negev Desert has cliffs and colorful canyons.

Wild goats called ibex (EYE-beks) live in the dry desert mountains.

north. The Rift Valley is a long strip of flat, low land in the east. The Jordan River, which flows through the valley, is Israel's longest river. It empties into the Dead Sea. That body of water is so salty that only a few plants and animals can live in it.

The Negev Desert makes up the southern half of Israel. Few people live in that hot, dry place.

Weather and Seasons

Israel is a small country. Still, the weather can be very different in the north and the south. Summers in Israel are hot and dry. The Sun shines most days from May through October. The hottest month is August, when temperatures can top 100° Fahrenheit (38° Celsius).

Did you know?

In spring and fall, hot, dry winds blow in dust from deserts in nearby countries.

Winters are cool and mild. January is the coldest month of the year. Hilly areas are cooler than the lowlands. Snow sometimes falls in the high mountains.

Even though much of Israel is hot and dry, snow sometimes falls in the mountains.

Every year, Israelis celebrate a special tree holiday. People plant trees to help keep the soil from blowing away.

The amount of rainfall varies a lot in different parts of the country. December is the rainiest month, especially in the northern hills. Thunderstorms are common.

The Negev Desert, in the south, is the driest area. Almost no rain falls there.

Israeli People

More than six million people live in Israel. Most of them are Jewish. They follow the laws of **Judaism**. That is one of the world's oldest religions. Some Jews follow strict rules about how to dress and what to eat. They pray three times a day. Other Jews do not follow such strict rules.

Arabs live in Israel, too. Most Arabs are Muslims. Muslims follow the religion of **Islam** and worship Allah. A few Arabs are Christians. **Christianity** is based on the life and teachings of Jesus Christ.

Both Arabs and Jews live in Israel, but the two groups are often divided. In most cities, they live in separate neighborhoods. They have different holidays and **customs**.

Jewish men wear prayer shawls at morning religious services.

The Western Wall
הכותל המערבי
حائط المبكى

Did you know?

Almost three million people visit Israel each year.

Signs are printed in Hebrew, Arabic, and English.

Muslims pray together on Fridays at noon. Some worshippers kneel on prayer mats.

Israel has two main languages, Hebrew and Arabic. Jewish people mostly speak Hebrew. Arabs mostly speak Arabic. Many people in Israel speak English, too.

School and Family

Children from the ages of five to sixteen must go to school. Almost all Muslim and Jewish children in Israel go to separate schools. Some schools are run by the government. Some are religious schools.

Students learn math, science, reading, and art. They study Hebrew or Arabic. Beginning in fifth or sixth grade, they learn English, too. Children go to school six days a week.

Muslim girls and boys usually go to separate schools.

Israeli students learn to use computers at school.

Did you know?

Muslim students do not go to school on Friday, because it is their holy day. Jewish students do not have classes on Saturday, their holy day.

Children help with chores around the house and on farms. This boy is carrying firewood.

A few Jewish and Arab students go to school together. They learn their lessons in both Arabic and Hebrew.

After school, many children play sports or take art or music lessons. At home, they help with chores. Most Jewish families are small. They have two or three children. Arab families are usually bigger. About half of all Jewish women work outside the home. Most Arab women do not.

Country Life

In the past, many people in Israel lived in the country. Today, few do. Most people who live in the country make their home on a **kibbutz**. A kibbutz is a place where several families live and work together. They work in farm fields or in **factories**.

Members of a kibbutz share the land and the business. Instead of being paid money, they often get food, housing, and schooling in exchange for work.

Many families live and work together on a large kibbutz.

Children on a kibbutz share the work, including caring for farm animals.

Did you know?

In the past, children on a kibbutz lived in a separate children's house. They spent just a few hours a day with their parents.

About one-third of Israel's farm goods come from a kibbutz.

Families live in separate houses on the kibbutz. All members eat meals together in a big dining room. Kids play together in a children's house after school.

Farmers on a kibbutz grow grains, fruits, and vegetables. They also raise goats, sheep, cows, and chickens. The children help with farm chores.

City Life

Most people in Israel live and work in cities. Jerusalem is home to the most people. Its streets are crowded with cars and buses. Parts of Jerusalem have new malls and modern office buildings. In older areas, outdoor markets line stone streets. The city has many places of worship.

Did you know?

Jerusalem is sometimes called "the City of Gold." Many buildings are made with a pink-white stone that looks golden in the sunshine.

Shoppers visit an outdoor market in Jerusalem.

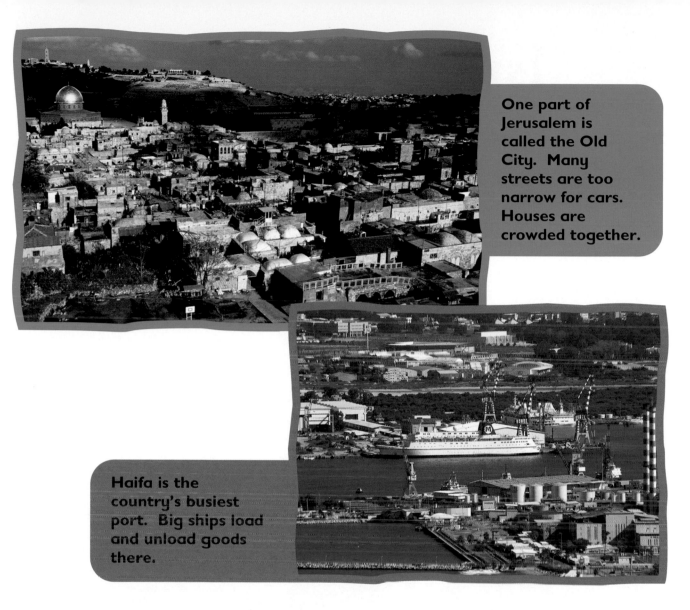

One part of Jerusalem is called the Old City. Many streets are too narrow for cars. Houses are crowded together.

Haifa is the country's busiest port. Big ships load and unload goods there.

The city is home to many holy places. Jews, Muslims, and Christians from all over the world come to visit them.

The second-biggest city is Tel Aviv. Tel Aviv is a modern city. It has tall buildings, sidewalk cafés, beaches, and museums. It is an important business center.

Haifa (HIGH-fah) is a major **port** on the coast of the Mediterranean Sea. Many goods are shipped in from and out to other countries. Elat is a busy port on the Red Sea.

Israeli Houses

In the cities, most people live in tall apartment buildings. They are usually made of stone, and many have a **balcony**. A balcony is an upper porch with a railing. In hot weather, people sometimes eat outside on balconies to keep cool.

People on a kibbutz live in small houses. The homes have white walls and red tile roofs. Some rich people in Israel live in large, fancy houses and apartments.

Many people live in high-rise apartment buildings in Israel's large cities.

Small houses with red tile roofs are common on a kibbutz.

Nomads move from place to place in the desert. They live in tents, which they carry with them.

In the desert, people called **nomads** move from place to place. They live in tents made of goat hair. Nomads take their tents with them when they travel to **graze** their goats and sheep. Camels carry the tents.

Israeli Food

People have come from many countries to live in Israel. They eat different kinds of foods. **Falafel** is a favorite Middle Eastern dish. It is fried chickpeas and spices in **pita** bread. Pita is a thin, flat bread made into a pocket.

People in Israel eat a lot of rice, fruits, and vegetables. Eggs, cheese, and bread are popular, too. Some people enjoy salad for breakfast. Lunch is usually the main meal of the day.

Falafel, or fried chickpeas in pita bread, is a popular dish.

Markets sell dried fruits grown by Israeli farmers.

People like eating in restaurants and cafés in Israel's cities.

Jewish families gather to eat holiday meals. They share special foods and say prayers.

Many Jewish people follow strict rules about food. For example, they do not eat pork. They follow Jewish food laws to prepare meals that are **kosher**. Most restaurants and hotels in Israel serve kosher foods.

Did you know?

During the Jewish holiday of Passover, Jews eat a kind of bread called **matzo**. It is flat, like a cracker.

At Work

Many people in Israeli cities work in banks, hotels, and shops. Some people teach school, write for newspapers, or have government jobs. Some are doctors or nurses.

In Israel, many scientists work to help people stay healthy. Others find new ways to move water to dry places so that farmers can grow food and flowers.

Some people work in factories. They make products such as paper, plastic goods, and clothing. Miners get salt and other **minerals** from the Dead Sea.

Workers remove salt from the Dead Sea. It is the world's saltiest lake.

Most of the world's diamonds pass through Israel. Workers there cut and polish the rough stones. Then they sell the cut diamonds to people in many countries.

Almost all Jewish men and most unmarried Jewish women must serve in the army, navy, or air force. They sign on at the age of eighteen. Men must serve for three years. Women serve for about two years.

Did you know?

Israel sells more cut diamonds than any other country.

This worker looks closely at a cut diamond.

Female soldiers train to serve in Israel's army. Military service is required of both men and women.

Having Fun

People in Israel like to go to the beach. Israel has a lot of pretty beaches on its long coastline. Swimming, boating, and windsurfing are popular activities. People also enjoy beach volleyball. **Matkot** is an Israeli beach tennis game.

Many people like team sports, too. They play and watch soccer and basketball. Jewish athletes from around the world come to Israel to play in the Maccabiah Games. The games are held every four years.

Many people in Israel enjoy the country's beautiful beaches.

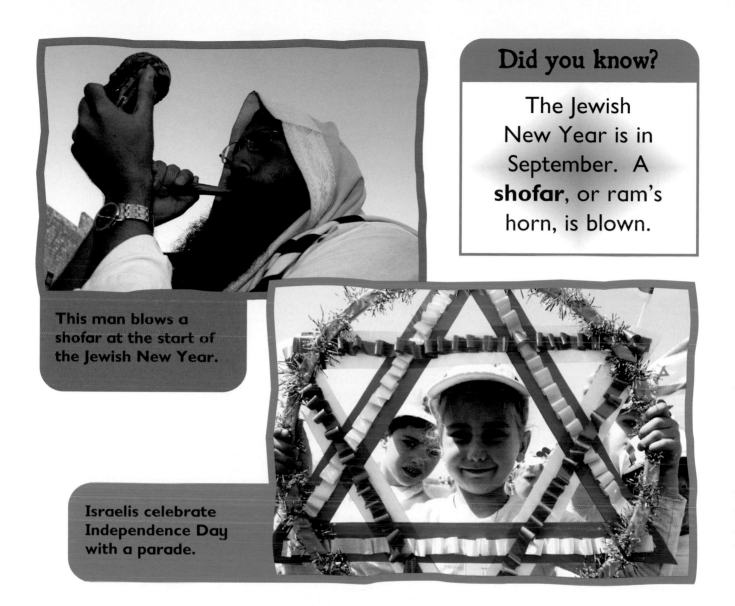

This man blows a shofar at the start of the Jewish New Year.

Israelis celebrate Independence Day with a parade.

People in Israel love to read, visit museums, and go to theaters. Israelis also enjoy playing and listening to music and dancing. Most children and teens join youth groups. The members enjoy picnics, plays, and other fun events. They also learn more about their country.

People take holidays, too. On Independence Day in May, they watch parades and fireworks. Jews, Muslims, and Christians celebrate religious holidays in special ways.

Israel: The Facts

• The official name of Israel is the State of Israel.

• Israel is a **democracy**. The people vote to elect government leaders.

• The **Knesset** is the lawmaking body. It has 120 elected members. The president has formal duties. The prime minister handles the day-to-day business of running the government.

• All citizens who are eighteen or older may vote in elections.

• Hebrew and Arabic are the languages of Israel.

The flag of Israel shows a blue Star of David in the middle. The star is a very old Jewish symbol.

The Israeli unit of money is the **shekel**.

Did you know?

Israel is small in land area. It is about the size of the state of New Jersey.

Jewish families celebrate Hanukkah (HAH-nuh-kuh), a holiday of lights.

Glossary

balcony – an upper porch with a railing

Christianity – the religion of Christians, based on the life and teachings of Jesus Christ

coastal plain – a flat area of land along an ocean or a sea

customs – traditions or usual ways of acting in a community or group

democracy – a government in which the people elect their leaders

factories – a building or group of buildings where goods are made

falafel – a popular Middle Eastern food made of fried chickpeas and spices in pita bread

graze – to put animals out to eat grass in fields

Islam – the religion of Muslims, who worship Allah

Judaism – the religion of the Jews, based on the Torah, the Jewish Bible

kibbutz – a farm or settlement in Israel where people live and work together

Knesset – the lawmaking body in Israel

kosher – foods that are made following Jewish food laws

matkot – a beach tennis game played in Israel

matzo – a flat bread eaten during Passover, a Jewish holiday

minerals – solid materials mined or dug from the ground, such as salt and diamonds

nomads – people who wander from place to place, living in tents and grazing their animals

pita – a thin, flat bread folded into a pocket

port – a town or city where goods are brought in and sent out on ships

shekel – the basic unit of money in Israel

shofar – a ram's-horn trumpet blown during Jewish holidays

Find Out More

Enchanted Learning.com

www.enchantedlearning.com/geography/mideast

Fact Monster: Israel

www.factmonster.com/ipkaA0107652.html

FunTrivia: Israel Quizzes

www.funtrivia.com/quizzes/geography/asia/israel.html

Kids Konnect: Israel Fast Facts

www.kidskonnect.com/Israel/IsraelHome.html

Publisher's note to educators and parents: Our editors have carefully reviewed these Web sites to ensure that they are suitable for children. Many Web sites change frequently, however, and we cannot guarantee that a site's future contents will continue to meet our high standards of quality and educational value. Be advised that children should be closely supervised whenever they access the Internet.

My Map of Israel

Photocopy or trace the map on page 31. Then write in the names of the countries, bodies of water, cities, land areas, and territories listed below. (Look at the map on page 5 if you need help).

After you have written in the names of all the places, find some crayons and color the map!

Countries
Egypt
Israel
Jordan
Lebanon
Syria

Bodies of Water
Dead Sea
Jordan River
Mediterranean Sea
Red Sea

Cities
Elat
Haifa
Jerusalem
Tel Aviv

Land Areas, Mountains, and Deserts
Mount Meron
Negev Desert
Rift Valley

Disputed Territories (lands fought over by Israelis and Arabs)
Gaza Strip
Golan Heights
West Bank

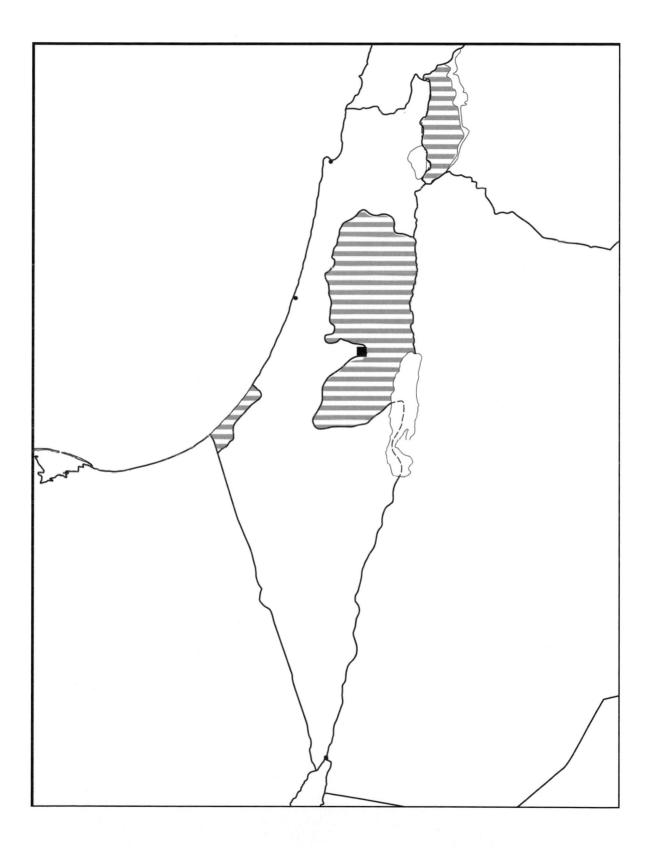

Index